MG 1965-1980
PHOTO ARCHIVE

MG 1965-1980
PHOTO ARCHIVE

David A. Knowles

Iconografix
Photo Archive Series

Iconografix
PO Box 609
Osceola, Wisconsin 54020 USA

Library of Congress Card Number 96-76221

ISBN 1-882256-53-0

96 97 98 99 00 5 4 3 2 1

Cover and book design by Lou Gordon, Osceola, Wisconsin

Printed in the United States of America

Book trade distribution by Voyageur Press, Inc. (800) 888-9653

PREFACE

The histories of machines and mechanical gadgets are contained in the books, journals, correspondence, and personal papers stored in libraries and archives throughout the world. Written in tens of languages, covering thousands of subjects, the stories are recorded in millions of words.

Words are powerful. Yet, the impact of a single image, a photograph or an illustration, often relates more than dozens of pages of text. Fortunately, many of the libraries and archives that house the words also preserve the images.

In the *Photo Archive Series*, Iconografix reproduces photographs and illustrations selected from public and private collections. The images are chosen to tell a story—to capture the character of their subject. Reproduced as found, they are accompanied by the captions made available by the archive.

The Iconografix *Photo Archive Series* is dedicated to young and old alike, the enthusiast, the collector and anyone, who like us, is fascinated by "things" mechanical.

ACKNOWLEDGMENTS

We wish to acknowledge the contributions of Denis Chick of Rover, Don Hayter, Paul Hughes, Bob Neville, Bob Owen, Graham Robson, Peter Rushforth, Tom Studer, and Dickie Wright.

The M.G. and Austin-Healey family photographed for the 1970 model year.

INTRODUCTION

The launch of the MGB, on September 20, 1962, heralded a further dramatic climb in the fortunes of M.G., which had already seen output rise to unprecedented levels. Even before the launch of the open MGB roadster, M.G. had formulated plans for a fixed-head coupé version. The project finally reached fruition in 1965, when the classically beautiful MGB GT was launched. Popular legend has it that Pininfarina was wholly responsible for the lines of the MGB GT. This was not strictly so. Jim Stimson of M.G. drew the basic lines, including the taller windscreen, which set the MGB GT apart from the roadster. Pininfarina, according to Stimson, sharpened up the shape and ensured that the end result looked so elegant.

The MGB GT was well received both at home and abroad. The M.G. factory, also pouring forth M.G. Midgets, MGB roadsters, and Austin-Healeys—not to mention the occasional Morris Minor Traveller—was recording healthy profits for British Motor Corporation (BMC). Behind the scenes at BMC's Longbridge headquarters, however, the cracks were beginning to show. Sir Leonard Lord (Lord Lambury), the autocratic head of the BMC combine since 1953, had stepped aside in favour of his heir apparent, Sir George Harriman. Whereas Lord had been able to impose his will upon the company, Harriman was less able to shape events. Contemporaries have suggested that, if anything, he was perhaps too much of a gentleman and not nearly ruthless enough. Many decisions by the company—often shaped by the brilliant but eccentric mind of Sir Alec Issigonis, creator of the Mini—appeared to defy logic. At first, this had no immediate bearing on the fortunes of M.G., but the emergence of the tragically flawed MGC of 1967—with its heavy and massive cast-iron engine—indicated that all was not well. Despite this, M.G. was establishing an impressive competition record, with notable successes at Le Mans, Monte Carlo, and Sebring.

In 1966, just as new safety and anti-pollution legislation was taking shape in the USA, BMC began a series of acquisitions and mergers; buying the Pressed Steel body manufacturers, and joining forces with Sir William Lyons' Jaguar Car Company. The resulting conglomerate was known as British Motor Holdings (BMH).

In January 1968 came an event which marked the beginning of a change in M.G.'s fortunes; a merger was announced between BMH and the Leyland Group. The resultant giant becoming British Leyland Motor Corporation (BLMC) in May 1968. For the first time, M.G. found themselves part of the same parent organisation as their deadly Triumph rivals. As it was managers from Triumph who swept into the corridors of power at Longbridge, M.G.'s fears were justified.

When Leyland effectively took control of M.G., it found that although Sir George Harriman and his managers had begun to deal with their many problems, it was a case of too little too late. Consequently, what had seemed at first to be a highly profitable dream marriage slipped rapidly towards the beginnings of a nightmare. At first, M.G. remained buoyant. Sales in the USA climbed from 37,000 in 1968 to over 51,000 in 1970—despite the increasing difficulty of funding and complying with the increasingly onerous demands of both the National Highway Safety Administration and the Environmental Protection Agency. North American manufacturers were better able to swallow these additional costs, due to their enormous production outputs and almost total dependence upon their home market for sales. BLMC—whose home market legislators would be at least twenty years behind their North American counterparts—were forced to absorb such costs against a much smaller number of increasingly outmoded and unique sports cars built chiefly for the USA.

In 1969, M.G. tried their hand at producing an all-new sports car. At first, "ADO21" was envisaged as a mid-engined M.G. Midget replacement. Before long, however, it had grown to become an intended replacement for the bigger-selling MGB. It is likely that this fact helped to seal its fate, for Sir Donald Stokes, head of BLMC, decreed that there would be only one new corporate sports car to replace the MGB and TR6—and that would eventually emerge in 1975 as the Triumph TR7.

By late 1970, ADO21 was dead. Yet, in July 1971, the TR7 would be given the green light for production at an all-new factory near Liverpool. In the meantime, M.G., with design being increasingly governed by cost-conscious former Ford UK personnel who had been recruited to Longbridge, suddenly "discovered" the 1970s. The 1970 model year Midget and MGB were face-lifted with styled steel wheels, bright colours, vinyl interior trim, and recessed matte black grilles. Those who defended these changes argued that they reflected what the North American market demanded. Such arguments were somewhat deflated when BLMC's North American off-shoot demanded the return of the chrome grille for 1973.

At this point, the men at Abingdon were allowed to create perhaps their finest post-war production sports car. The MGB GT V8 saw the lovely 215 cubic-inch (3,528 c.c.), all-aluminium former Buick V8 engine, which the Rover Car Company had acquired from General Motors in 1964, shoe-horned into the engine bay of the equally lovely MGB GT body. The result was a firecracker which could top 125 mph and reach 60 mph from rest in under eight seconds. Sadly, the MGB

GT V8 was denied the North American sales which it so richly deserved. Produced for less than four years, only 2,591 units were built, and in the USA, where only a handful of early cars went, it took on an almost mythical status.

The next series of shocks to jolt M.G. began in October 1974. The entire M.G. sports car family—Midget, MGB, MGB GT, and MGB GT V8—received smoothly styled black polyurethane bumpers, in response to the latest "no damage" legislation imposed in the USA. M.G. enthusiasts were outraged, but even more so when they found that the trusty A-series engine of the Midget had been phased out in favour of a Triumph unit. Soon afterwards, in January 1975, the MGB GT was withdrawn from sale in the USA, simultaneously making way for the Triumph TR7. The surviving US-market MGB lost its classic twin SU carburettors in favour of a single Stromberg unit. As emissions legislation tightened, the MGB's ageing B-series engine became ever more constricted and lethargic. By the end of the 1970s, its performance figures became something of an embarrassment.

Plans to fit the all-new O-series engine to US-bound MGBs were posted and then abandoned. This was an on-and-off process throughout the 1970s, as the parent company lurched from crisis to crisis, almost collapsing in 1974 and only being saved by government intervention the following year. In May 1979, Britain elected a new Conservative Government, under the powerful leadership of Margaret Thatcher. Boosted by this news, the UK stock-market soared, and the Pound Sterling climbed rapidly against the Dollar. Embattled British Leyland, already struggling to make ends meet and trying to tackle the legacy of years of poor industrial relations, had been under the direction of Sir Michael Edwardes since November 1977. The reaction of Edwardes and his team to the shift in exchange rates was to announce the discontinuation of the MGB in September 1979 and to plan to concentrate dwindling sports car resources on Triumph and Jaguar. For a time, a consortium led by Aston Martin appeared to offer hope for the MGB, but these ambitions came to nothing. The M.G. plant itself was to close by the end of October 1980. Plans to offer an M.G.-badged version of the TR7 briefly surfaced in December 1980, but by the beginning of 1981 these ideas too had been abandoned. And so, the *Sports Car America Loved First* was laid to rest.

M.G. 1965-1980 Photo Archive presents a comprehensive collection of M.G. models, prototypes, race and rally cars. The photographs are reproduced, for the most part, in chronological order.

The major M.G. event of 1965 was
the launch at the Earls Court Motor
Show of the beautiful MGB GT.

12

The MGB GT married the attractive lines of the MGB with a crisp, elegant Pininfarina detailed roof line—a true classic of automotive styling.

An early home-market MGB.

Justly proud of the MGB GT, Chief Engineer Syd Enever poses alongside a home-market specimen, whilst in the background, US export MGBs await despatch.

Paddy Hopkirk and Andrew Hedges drove this MGB in the factory's last entry at Le Mans, June 1965. Their average speed was 98.25 mph over 2,357.95 miles.

The Austin-Healey 3000 Mk. IV prototype of 1966, codenamed AD052, shows the attempt to marry the distinctive Austin-Healey 3000 grille with the nose of the MGB. Donald Healey would not sanction the use of his name on this car and so it was abandoned.

This is not a photograph taken inside the Abingdon M.G. factory. It is, in fact, the Pressed Steel Fisher assembly plant at Swindon. J. Yeates is shown fitting the windscreen finishers to an MGB GT Mark I—something of a black art! At this time, roadster bodies were painted and trimmed at a different factory in Coventry, which explains why these are all MGB GTs.

For the April 1967 Sebring 12-Hour Race, BMC prepared a lightweight MGB GT, seen here at Abingdon during the course of preparation.

The MGB GT, still bearing its UK registration LBL 591E, roars around the Sebring circuit in April 1967.

Paddy Hopkirk in LBL 591E chases a Porsche at Sebring.

MBL 546E later became one of the famous lightweight MGC GTS factory duo. Initially, prior to the MGC launch, it was raced as a prototype with a 2,004 c.c. MGB engine and a normal MGB bonnet. It is seen here prior to the Targa Florio of May 1967.

EX234 with Hydrolastic suspension, which was planned to replace both the Midget and the MGB, survives today in the collection of Syd Beer.

This Pininfarina bodied prototype was EX234, a fully finished road-worthy prototype. Pretty though it was, it stood no chance during the turbulent years before and after the BL merger.

The MGC GT made its debut on the M.G. stand at the October 1967 Motor Show.

The heart of the MGC's problem—the heavy cast-iron straight six engine.

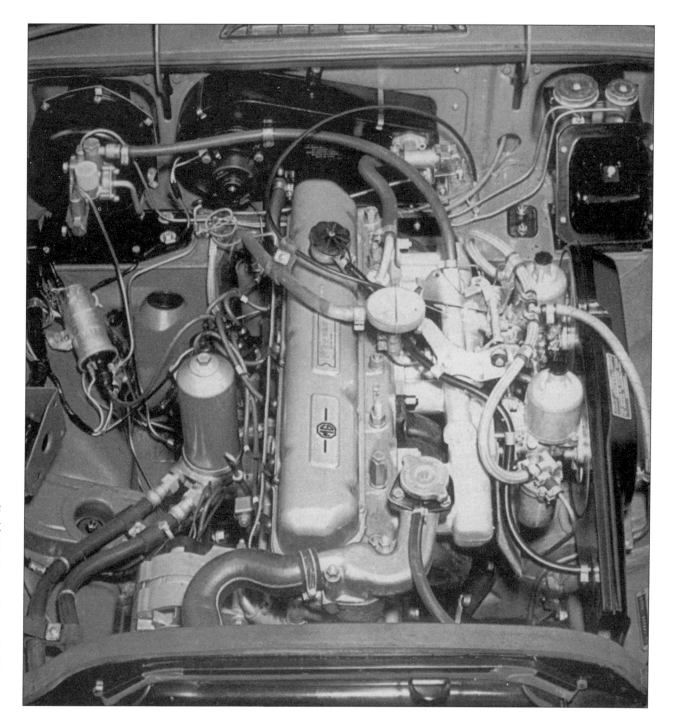

Installation of the massive straight six engine necessitated many changes to the engine bay of the MGC, in comparison to the MGB. The radiator was moved forward, and the front suspension—just visible in this photo—was completely new.

Launched at the same time as the MGC was the Rover V8 engine. Newly acquired from General Motors, it had been dropped from the Buick Skylark in 1964. This is the installation in a 1968 Rover 3.5 P5B, which makes an interesting comparison with the Costello car shown later.

An early home-market MGC GT, showing the larger (fifteen inch diameter) wheels and the controversial bonnet bulge.

One rather famous customer who acquired an MGC GT was His Royal Highness Prince Charles, soon to become the Duke of Wales. His car received some extra special attention at the factory. It now resides in the Royal Museum at Sandrigham, HRH having switched his allegiance to Aston Martins.

An aerial view of the M.G. factory in 1968, looking west towards the nearby village of Marcham.

M.G. Midgets and Austin-Healey Sprites proceeding down the line in 1968. In the foreground are right-hand drive cars. The parallel line just visible in the background carries left-hand drive cars.

USA specification M.G. Midgets and Austin-Healey Sprites going down the line. Note the engine-driven air-pump, the triple windscreen wipers, and side reflectors, which identify these as 1969 model year cars. The front car is a Sprite, the next a Midget.

In the foreground is a US-specification M.G. Midget, whilst following closely behind at the Abingdon factory is a US-specification Austin-Healey Sprite.

MBL 546E, one of the two factory MGC GTS racers, pictured at Sebring in March 1968.

In June 1968, just after the BL/BMH merger, the factory entered the two MGC GTS cars in the Marathon de la Route. This is "Mabel"—MBL 546E—thundering around the Nürburgring circuit. Note the wire wheels. Minilites had been tried in testing, but were abandoned on MBL 546E although the other car, RMO 699F, ran on Minilites.

The M.G. 1300 Mk. II.

The M.G. 1300 Mk. II was the first time that the UK market saw the two-door version of the ADO16. It had been available in the USA since 1962.

Engine bay of the M.G. 1300 Mk. II of 1968/9.

The interior of the M.G. 1300 Mk. II saloon was tastefully appointed. This is a Continental European specification car. Note the left-hand steering wheel and kilometres-per-hour speedometer.

The interior of the home-market right-hand drive version of the M.G. 1300 Mk. II. Note the attractive figured walnut of the fascia.

By 1969, the future of the MGC was looking bleak. Bruce McWilliams of British Leyland's North America office experimented with ways to spice up the styling.

For a very short time, the M.G. Midget and contemporary Austin-Healey Sprite featured a black windscreen surround, as seen on this 1970 model year car.

This is a very confused M.G. Midget; it is right-hand drive, yet features US-market rear lamp clusters and an M.G. 1300 steering wheel!

In this view, the M.G. grille badge and "Midget" chrome sill script can be clearly seen. For the Austin-Healey Sprite, there was little more to distinguish it than different badges.

Between 1969 and 1971, the M.G. Midget and Austin-Healey Sprite featured this unique pressed-steel wheel.

The US-market M.G. Midget for 1970, photographed in 1969. Note the square licence plate backing, side marker lights, triple windscreen wipers, and single driver's door mirror.

The interior of the US-specification 1970 model year M.G. Midget, in this case fitted with the wrong steering wheel type. Note the heavily padded dashboard and standard fit head restraints.

The 1970 model year US-specification MGB also featured a padded dashboard with no glove box. Note the use of rocker switches and the fixed type seat belts, anchored through the hood tonneau.

A pre-production US-specification 1970 model year MGB roadster photographed for publicity purposes. This car features Mark I style curved red rear lenses, rather than the correct squarer pattern ones fitted in production. Note the short-lived split rear quarter bumpers.

Automatic transmission was offered for a while on MGBs, but not in the USA. This is a home-market MGB GT. Note the neat selector quadrant and the illumination lamp fixed below the fascia.

The MGB GT for the 1970 model year. The steering wheel, fitted to this car for photographic purposes, is wrong. The boss with chrome finished M.G. badge suggests that it is in fact an M.G. 1300 wheel.

A 1970 model year home-market M.G. Midget at speed. The black screen surround is rare—common in publicity photographs but rare on production cars. Note the driver's head-gear!

M.G. had dramatic plans for the 1970s, as this Paul Hughes/Harris Mann styled prototype ADO21 shows.

ADO21 was no less remarkable from the rear. It was to have been a mid-engined car, with a potential choice of 1,498 and 1,748 c.c. four cylinder engines or a 2,227 c.c. six.

MGB, Midget, and M.G. 1300 Mk. II at the 1970 Earls Court Motor Show.

A prototype US-specification 1971 model year MGB GT photographed at Longbridge in November 1969.

Front end of the prototype MGB GT, showing the controversial recessed grille.

This rear view of the prototype MGB GT shows the oversized head-restraints and a prototype of the later US dashboard, without the quilted padding in front of the passenger.

Throughout production, in any guise, the MGB GT always remained supremely elegant, especially from the rear three-quarter view as here.

This prototype MGB roadster was fitted with similar oversized head-restraints to its GT counterpart. Note the steering wheel with perforated flat silver spokes.

The M.G. Midget continued with the controversial "black hole" grille until 1974. This is a 1971/2 car.

For 1971 into 1972, M.G. continued with the black grille, as seen on this MGB roadster.

A home-market 1973 model year MGB interior, of late 1972. Note the open-slotted steering wheel. These slots would soon be filled in because of safety concerns.

The elegant lines of the classic MGB GT—in this case, a home-market 1973 model year car.

In 1972, Kent-based engineer and Mini racer Ken Costello started building his Costello MGB V8 conversions in modest but regular quantities.

British Leyland were very interested in the Costello MGB V8, so they asked Ken Costello to send one to M.G. for study. This photo shows how the ex-Buick Rover 3.5 Litre V8 unit fitted neatly into the MGB engine bay.

One thing about which M.G. were not convinced was the large bulge in the Costello's fibre-glass bonnet, a legacy of the standard Rover's centrally mounted SU carburettors.

M.G. were very critical of the Costello's conversion. Notes by M.G.'s Don Hayter on the reverse of this photo state "exhaust close to clutch, flexible hose, solenoid and harness wires and B-series gearbox."

An MGB GT V8 (the air filter is just visible!) during crash-testing at 30 mph into a steel-faced concrete cube at Abingdon. The disc-like object at bottom right is a timing device, driven by a precisely calibrated electric motor to enable the high-speed film to be accurately timed.

Two views of a late-1973/early-1974 home-market MGB roadster. Notice the fashions current at the time.

Still elegant after eight years in production, the MGB GT took on new purpose with the addition of the V8 engine in August 1973.

Launched on August 15, 1973, the MGB GT V8 was the most powerful M.G. sports car ever built, not eclipsed until the M.G. RV8 of 1992.

The MGB GT V8 at speed on the A420 Oxford to Swindon road. The registration number is false.

HOH 902L pictured on test, probably in Richmond Park, south-west London.

The distinctive air filters of the MGB GT V8 were known as "lobster claws." This is an early press car. Later cars did not have the rather superfluous radiator fan guard brazed onto the top of this early car's radiator. Note the twin electric fans just visible ahead of the radiator!

A prototype MGB GT V8 engine to North American Federal specification. Only a few were built, as the car was only sold in the UK.

HOH 933L was tested by *Motor* magazine, who achieved a top speed of 125 mph and a 0-60 mph time of 7.7 seconds, both pretty impressive figures in 1973. It is now owned by collector Syd Beer.

One of the few means of recognising the MGB GT V8 in your rear view mirror.

Ken Costello did not rest on his laurels. His Mark 2 Costello MGB GT V8 featured Weber carburetion, which allowed retention of the standard MGB bonnet. Note the distinctive Costello radiator grille.

The MGB GT V8 was tested by many British and European magazines. This is one of the press fleet.

The M.G. Midget of 1973/4 still retained the black grille introduced with the 1970 model year.

Interior of the home-market M.G. Midget for 1974.

Interior of the MGB GT V8.

Close up of the dashboard of the MGB GT V8.

A very rare beast indeed—one of only seven "production" left-hand drive US-specification MGB GT V8s built. This car is chassis number GD2D2-DUD-102G, photographed after restoration in 1990. There were also two pre-production cars, making nine left-hand drive US-specification examples in all.

The distinctive Dunlop composite steel/alloy wheel fitted to the MGB GT V8.

A home-market "Rubber Bumper" MGB of late 1974. Note the body colour front valance that was soon changed to satin black.

Announced in the UK on October 16, 1974, was the "Rubber Bumper" M.G. Midget with the Triumph 1500 engine.

Few M.G. enthusiasts welcomed this sight in late 1974—a Triumph Spitfire engine in an M.G. was almost sacriligeous! This is a twin-SU carburettor home-market car.

In the USA, the relative rarity of the Rover 3.5 Litre engine and the unavailability of the factory MGB GT V8 prompted private individuals to experiment with the alloy Rover engine's Buick and Oldsmobile ancestors. This car has a turbocharged Oldsmobile unit.

Early 1974 saw the retirement of another of M.G.'s legendary team. Here Alec Hounslow (in foreground) shakes the hand of Don Hayter. The car is the prototype right-hand drive MGB GT V8, chassis number GD2D1-99G.

This photograph, taken in 1974, shows, left to right, Don Hayter, Syd Enever, secretary Isla Watts, and Roy Brocklehurst, on the occasion of Isla's retirement. Syd had been retired for three years and Roy had handed over the reins at Abingdon to Don the previous year.

A 1975 model year MGB GT V8, complete with the impact absorbing bumpers required by the North American market. It was rather ironic that the V8 was never exported to the USA!

This low-angle shot perhaps does the MGB GT V8 no favours.

1975 model year MGB GT V8. Note the body colour front apron, later changed to satin black.

Rear view of the 1975 model year MGB GT V8, launched on October 16, 1974.

A European specification left-hand drive MGB roadster with chrome Rostyle wheels.

The MGB GT counterpart. The satin black front valance (below the bumper) and the small black and chrome C pillar flash denote this as a 1976 model year car. By this point, the MGB GT had been dropped from the USA but it continued on sale in the UK right through to the end.

In the USA, M.G. launched this M.G. Midget Special, with standard AM/FM radio, chrome luggage rack, chrome wheel trim rims, and a distinctive side stripe.

In 1975, in an attempt to harmonise the lines of the bumpers with the bodywork, BL stylist Rob Owen produced this rendering as an idea for a facelifted MGB GT.

The home-market M.G. range for the 1976 model year. Note the black front valances.

The interior of the home-market MGB and MGB GT for the 1977 model year onwards featured these gaudy striped fabric seats. Originally designed for the US market, they were never sent there once it was realised that the customers did not want such trim. Note the striped headrests on this pre-production prototype. Production cars had black vinyl headrests.

A 1977 model year home-market MGB roadster.

During 1976, Leyland Cars supported this privately run MGB GT V8 entry by Stratstone, a major British distributor of BL vehicles.

The Stratstone MGB GT V8 was driven by Mike Gidden, Tim Goss, and former M.G. apprentice Bob Neville.

Another intrepid MGB GT V8 campaigner was Peter Rushforth, seen here with Michael Pearson-Kirk piloting one of the left-hand drive early production cars (GD2D2-DUD-102G) on the Lombard RAC Rally, November 27-30, 1976.

Peter Rushforth is seen here driving his left-hand drive MGB GT V8 on the 1976 Palladwr Rally in Wales.

Another to put his faith in the V8 was Brian Field, who raced a pre-production left-hand drive prototype, GD2D2-97G. Brian converted the car to right-hand drive but retained all the original parts to allow it to be restored. This car was still in rally trim in 1996!

Peter Rushforth out again in HUD 578N on the 1977 International Welsh Rally.

The Stratstone MGB GT V8 makes its World International Championship debut at Silverstone, May 1977. Sadly the car failed to finish.

The second World International outing for the Stratstone MGB GT V8 was at Brands Hatch. It is seen here prior to the race.

The Stratstone MGB GT V8 is seen here at an extremely wet Brands Hatch in September 1977.

Despite the appalling conditions, the Stratstone car managed to achieve sixteenth place against strong opposition.

Malcolm Beer, son of well-known M.G. collector Syd, bought this MGB GT V8 racer from Bob Neville in 1977 and raced it for many years afterwards, winning many M.G. Car Club races.

In 1978, these attractive alloy wheels were offered as an optional extra. Similar wheels would later be fitted as standard on the final US-market MGB LE models. Note the prototype Rover SD1 estate car in the background of this Longbridge studio shot of September 1977.

A 1979 model year home-market MGB GT coupé, registered in August 1978. Later MGBs would lose the square BL badge just visible ahead of the door. The rectangular buffer at the back edge of the door would normally be removed upon delivery.

In June 1979, an exhibition was staged at the old Abingdon Gaol museum celebrating 50 years of association between the town and the M.G. factory. M.G. provided this crash-test car for public viewing outside the museum entrance.

Just prior to the announcement that the M.G. factory was to be closed, the author was able to visit the factory and took his camera with him. This is a batch of Japanese-market Midgets going down the line.

A Midget body being transferred between the two assembly decks.

This is a fairly late home-market M.G. Midget, judging by the "T" suffix to the registration plate, signifying registration between August 1978 and July 1979.

Syd Enever, by now nine years into retirement, made a special visit to the M.G. factory to help celebrate the production of the 500,000th MGB in January 1980.

Following the shock announcement by BLMC that the MGB was to be discontinued, a consortium led by Aston Martin prepared a bid for the name, car, and factory. To prove the seriousness of their intent, they enlisted stylist William Towns to facelift the MGB. Here are two of his sketches.

J. K. Martin of Aston Martin took this photograph of the Aston Martin MGB. Note the taller MGB GT windscreen and side glasses.

This is the end result photographed after the initial public debut. As first shown, the grille surround was chrome rather than satin black. The car still survives in private ownership.

While the Aston Martin consortium tried to acquire M.G., BLMC were looking at other ideas. This is one of a number of competing exercises, in this case by Triumph Engineering, to attempt to make an M.G. out of a TR7.

The rear of the Triumph Engineering "M.G. TR7" featured, in common with rival offerings, Rover SD1 tail lights. The idea was abandoned in January 1981.

In the meantime, M.G. were readying their final Limited Edition MGB swansong models. This photograph, taken by the author in late 1980, shows MGB LE and MGB GT LE bodies about to enter the factory. Note how complete the bodies already look at this stage!

The Iconografix Photo Archive Series includes:

The Iconografix Photo Archive Series is available from direct mail specialty book dealers and bookstores worldwide, or can be ordered from the publisher. For additional information or to add your name to our mailing list contact:

Iconografix
PO Box 609/Bk
Osceola, Wisconsin 54020 USA

Telephone: (715) 294-2792
(800) 289-3504 (USA)
Fax: (715) 294-3414

Book trade distribution by Voyageur Press, Inc., PO Box 338, Stillwater, Minnesota 55082 USA (800) 888-9653
European distribution by Midland Publishing Limited, 24 The Hollow, Earl Shilton, Leicester LE9 7N1 England

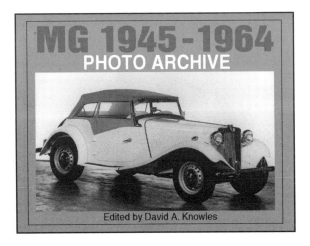

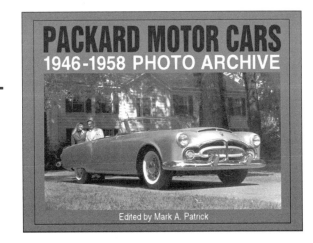

MORE
GREAT BOOKS FROM
ICONOGRAFIX

MG 1945-1964 *Photo Archive*
ISBN 1-882256-53-0

PACKARD MOTOR CARS 1946-1958
Photo Archive
ISBN 1-882256-45-X

SEBRING 12-HOUR RACE 1970
Photo Archive ISBN 1-882256-20-4

**LE MANS 1950: THE BRIGGS
CUNNINGHAM CAMPAIGN**
Photo Archive ISBN 1-882256-21-2

MACK MODEL B 1953-66 VOLUME 1
Photo Archive ISBN 1-882256-19-0

**COCA-COLA: A HISTORY IN PHOTO-
GRAPHS 1930-1969** *Photo Archive*
ISBN 1-882256-46-8

**AMERICAN SERVICE STATIONS
1935-1943** *Photo Archive*
ISBN 1-882256-27-1

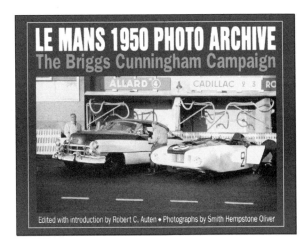

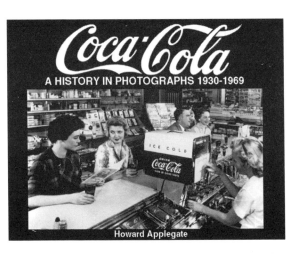

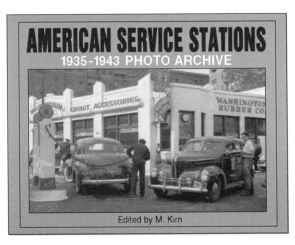